I0626898

Sumayyah

Stories of the Companions of the Prophet
Muhammad for Young Readers

By: Dr. A. Hannibal Hamdallahi

BLACK HEROES OF ISLAM SERIES

Sumayyah
Copyright © 2025 Sokoto Publishing

All rights reserved. No part of this publication may be reproduced, stored in a retrieval system, or transmitted in any form or by any means—electronic, mechanical, photocopying, recording, or otherwise—without the prior written permission of the publisher, except in the case of brief quotations embodied in critical articles or reviews.

This book is a work of creative storytelling and is intended to educate and inspire young readers about the life of Sumayyah, the first martyr of Islam. It is dedicated to all children who seek courage, faith, and inspiration from the heroes of our past.

First Edition: 2025
Published by Sokoto Publishing
Printed in the United States of America

For information about permissions, special editions, or bulk orders, please contact:
Sokoto Publishing
P.O. Box 280350
Nashville, TN 37228, USA
Email: info@sokotopublishing.com

Dedication

Since you left, I haven't been the same. May Allah grant you the highest level of Jannah. I look forward to the day I meet God and reunite with you, my dear Brother.

Today, we have the freedom to worship as Muslims without being harassed. But this freedom didn't come easy. It took the courage and dedication of men and women, to push society to accept it.

During Islam's beginning years, things were not easy for some of the early Believers. In fact, life was almost unbearable. Believers were harassed, embarrassed, humiliated, and tortured.

The leaders of the powerful Quraish tribe in Mecca, issued a general call to pressure Muslims in order to turn them away from their faith. This meant that members of the Quraish, and all of their affiliated tribes, clans, sects, and allies, were to attack and humiliate the Muslims to try to stop them from worshipping Allah.

Many Muslims during this period were brutally hurt and abused by the Quraish tribe. One woman's story has become legendary because of her steadfast faith and belief in Allah, and because of her ultimate sacrifice in the name of Islam.

This is Sumayyah bint Khayyat, or otherwise known simply as Sumayyah. Sumayyah was a freed woman from Abyssinia. She was freed after her marriage to Yasir, an Arab. But because Yasir was very poor, and Sumayyah was once a slave, they had little protection against the Quraish tribe who wanted to hurt the Muslims. Sumayyah, Yasir, and their son Ammar, were all brutally tortured as the Quraish wanted them to worship idols instead of Allah.

One day, members from the Quraish dragged Sumayyah and her family out into the heat, and hurt them very badly. They told them that all they had to do was denounce Islam, and speak well of the idol gods. Each time they asked Sumayyah to do this, she would refuse.

One of these brutal men, named Abu Jahl and uncle of Prophet Muhammad, said that he wanted her husband Yasir to see her tortured. Rather than give him the satisfaction of seeing her sweat, she spat in his face. Afterwards, Abu Jahl, who was a big enemy of Prophet Muhammad, thrust a spear through her body and she passed away.

إِنَّا لِلَّهِ وَإِنَّا إِلَيْهِ رَاجِعُونَ

Verily we belong to Allah, and verily to Him do we return.

This courageous Black woman and Companion of the Messenger of Allah, was the first martyr of Islam. She was the first person to die for her belief in Allah and for her refusal to worship idol gods.

Sumayyah's maytrdom became famous and served as a source of inspiration for many Muslims. When news of her martyrdom reached other Believers, they became even more devoted to the cause of Islam.

We continue to cherish the memory of Sumayyah today for her sacrifice and courage. Her dedication to Allah and the Holy Prophet continues to inspire generations of young Muslims today, just as she did for many of Islam's earliest Companions.

www.ingramcontent.com/pod-product-compliance
Lightning Source LLC
Chambersburg PA
CBHW041613120626

46551CB00002B/424